anythin

D0744319

REAL-LIFE ZOMBIES

EDGE BOOKS

BODY SNATCHERS

FLIES, WASPS,

AND OTHER CREEPY CRAWLY ZOMBIE MAKERS

BY JOAN AXELROD-CONTRADA

CONSULTANT:
BEN HANELT
RESEARCH ASSISTANT, PROFESSOR, AND LECTURER
DEPARTMENT OF BIOLOGY
UNIVERSITY OF NEW MEXICO
ALBUQUERQUE, NEW MEXICO

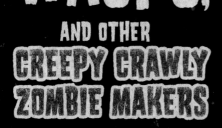

CAPSTONE PRESS
a capstone imprint

Edge Books are published by Capstone Press,
1710 Roe Crest Drive, North Mankato, Minnesota 56003
www.mycapstone.com

Cataloging-in-Publication Data
Cataloging-in-Publication Data is on file with the Library of Congress.
ISBN 978-1-5157-2480-3 (library binding)
ISBN 978-1-5157-2507-7 (eBook PDF)

Editorial Credits
Abby Colich, editor; Kyle Grenz, designer; Pam Mitsakos, media researcher; Laura
Manthe, production specialist

Photo Credits
Getty Images: Anand Varma, 16, 22, SMC Images, 13, Visuals Unlimited, Inc./
John Abbott, 6-7; Newscom: Europics, 19; Science Source: Emanuele Biggi/FLPA,
10-11; Shutterstock: Anest, 1, bmf-foto.de, cover, 17, Borkin Vadim, 29, Cosmin
Manci, 20-21 bottom middle, D. Kucharski K. Kucharska, 28, Dr. Morley Read, 15,
Henrik Larsson, back cover, IfH, 5, InsectWorld, 26-27, jack perks, 24-25, kurt_G,
4, plenoym, 20 top left, Protasov AN, 8; Wikimedia: Core A, Runckel C, Ivers J,
Quock C, Siapno T, et al. (2012). "A new threat to honey bees, the parasitic phorid
fly Apocephalus borealis". PLoS ONE 7 (1). DOI:10.1371/journal.pone.0029639.
Retrieved on 04 January 2012, 9

Design elements: Shutterstock

Printed in the United States of America.
009680F16

TABLE OF CONTENTS

NATURE'S ZOMBIES

In the tropics of Thailand, a fast-moving creature stumbles in a daze. It has just been stabbed in the brain.

Stripped of all free will, the victim has no control over its own actions.

Sound like a scene from a horror film? Perhaps, but it's the true tale of the jewel wasp, a ruthless parasitoid, and its victim, the cockroach.

jewel wasp

parasitoid—a parasite that kills its host

In the movies zombies are humans that rise from the dead. They walk the Earth with no control over their own actions. Zombies aren't real, but nature is full of creatures that act like them. When a parasite invades its host, the host no longer makes its own decisions. It lives under the control of its invader.

Decide for yourself. Are these body snatchers wonders of the Earth? Or nature's creepiest outlaws?

FAST FACT Parasites live on or in their hosts. Often parasites are harmless. Parasitoids go a step farther. They eventually kill their hosts.

parasite—an animal or plant that lives on or inside another animal or plant
host—a living plant or animal on which a parasite lives

ZOMBIE FIRE ANTS

Fire ants live in South America and parts of North America. Tiny phorid flies swoop down from the sky. They land on the ants. A female fly injects her eggs into an ant's chest. The eggs hatch inside. Tiny larvae travel to the ant's brain. Then the larvae slurp up the brain.

This turns the ant into a zombie.

carpenter ant

phorid fly

Fire ants usually stick with their group. But a mind-controlled ant marches away. It can wander aimlessly for up to two weeks.

Then the larvae cause the ant's head to fall off.

The fly larvae pupate inside the detached head. The young flies grow into adults. They fly away, later looking for their own fire ant hosts.

Insect Life Cycles

Why do zombie-makers control their hosts? They often use their hosts for protection during one or more stages of their life cycle. In some life cycles, insects hatch from eggs. The young insects look similar to how they will as adults. Other insects go through a longer life cycle. This cycle has four stages—egg, larva, pupa, and adult. A butterfly is an example of this cycle. From an egg, a caterpillar hatches. A caterpillar is a type of larva. The larva eats and grows until it enters the pupa stage. In this stage, the pupa develops inside a cocoon. When fully grown, it emerges as an adult butterfly.

larva—a stage of an insect's life between egg and adult
pupate—the process in which an insect changes from a larva into an adult
life cycle—the series of changes a living thing goes through from birth to death

ZOM-BEES

Late at night, a swarm of honeybees leave their hive. Normally the bees gather food during the day. But these zombies make a beeline for downtown streetlights.

It's as if an invisible force controls them.

honeybee

Then their actions become even stranger. The bees stumble around in circles. They try to stand on their legs, but can't.

Honeybees in Trouble

Today there are fewer honeybees in North America than there once were. Pesticides meant for other insects are partly to blame. Phorid flies may be another cause of the decline. Although phorid flies attack other kinds of bees, scientists didn't observe them infecting honeybees until 2008. Scientists aren't sure why the flies are now invading this new host.

Soon the bees drop dead. Larvae crawl out of their lifeless bodies.

The larvae are those of phorid flies. The flies inject eggs into bumblebees, yellow jacket hornets, and honeybees. The eggs develop into larvae inside their host. The larvae feed on the bees' insides. Scientists think the larvae change the bees' inner clock. Instead of visiting flowers by day, the honeybees leave their hives at night. This leads to the bees' death. About a week after the bees die, the larvae emerge and pupate.

phorid fly

swarm—to gather or fly close together in a large group

pesticide—a poisonous chemical used to kill insects, rats, and fungi that can damage plants

THE ZOMBIE-MAKING JEWEL WASP

In Africa, southern Asia, and the Pacific islands, a female jewel wasp stalks her next victim. A fast-moving cockroach crosses her path.

The cockroach is six times larger than the wasp. But the cockroach doesn't stand a chance. The wasp stings its victim. The cockroach can no longer move. The wasp injects venom. The venom helps control the cockroach. The wasp has turned it into a mindless zombie.

The cockroach, normally feisty, becomes calm. The wasp grabs it by the antenna. Then she walks it like a dog on a leash into a burrow. The wasp lays an egg on the cockroach. Then the wasp fills in the burrow with pebbles. She doesn't want any predators getting to her egg. Soon the egg hatches into a larva. The larva chews its way into the cockroach.

Then it eats the cockroach alive!

Later the wasp bursts out as an adult. The cockroach dies.

Dementor Wasps

A team of German scientists recently discovered a new wasp. In the rain forests of Thailand, the wasps put cockroaches into a zombielike state similar to the way the jewel wasp does. The black and red wasp needed a name. Researchers asked the public. Voters chose the dementor wasp. They named it for the soul-sucking Dementors in J.K. Rowling's Harry Potter books.

FAST FACT Cockroaches are pests to people all over the world. In Hawaii farmers use jewel wasps to protect sugar-cane plants from the pesky bugs.

venom—a poisonous liquid produced by some animals

burrow—a hole in the ground made or used by an animal

predator—an animal that hunts other animals for food

THE ZOMBIE ORB SPIDER

Near a leafy spot in Costa Rica, a wasp dives down onto an orb spider. The wasp lays an egg. The egg sticks to the spider. The wasp flies off and never returns. From the egg, a larva hatches.

Then the larva turns the spider into a web-weaving zombie.

Under the larva's control, the spider tears down its own sticky web. In its place the spider spins a new one just for the larva. The web is similar to the one the spider used when it molted. But the new web is even stronger. It's built to last longer for the larva. Scientists think that the larva flips a switch in the spider's brain that deals with molting. The behavior is already in place, but now it serves the wasp instead of the spider.

molt—to shed an outer layer of skin

wasp larva attached to an orb spider

How does the wasp larva return the favor? By eating the spider!

After its meal the larva pupates, using the spider web for its cocoon. Safe inside its spider-silk home, the pupa grows into an adult.

THE HEAD-BANGING ZOMBIE CATERPILLAR

From its perch in a Brazilian rain forest, a female wasp pounces on a helpless caterpillar. Then it injects about 80 eggs into the caterpillar's body. The eggs hatch into larvae. The larvae chomp away at the insides of the caterpillar. They take care not to destroy the caterpillar's **vital organs**.

They need the caterpillar to stay alive—for now!

As the larvae grow, the caterpillar blows up like a balloon. Then the larvae gnaw their way out of their host's skin.

vital organ—a body part needed to stay alive

The caterpillar now acts like a zombie possessed. It violently bangs its head. This scares away any of the wasps' predators. The larvae spin their pupae outside their host. The caterpillar stands guard. Several days later the wasps emerge as adults. Then the caterpillar finally dies.

wasp larvae attached to a caterpillar

FAST FACT

Scientists studied the bodies of these caterpillars. They found something interesting inside. Not all wasp larvae made it out alive. One or two stayed behind. Scientists think they controlled the caterpillar. They worked their way into the caterpillar's brain to keep their brothers and sisters safe.

parasitoid wasp

ZOMBIE LADYBUGS

An eerie scene unfolds in backyards and farms all over the world. A tiny female wasp inserts her stinger into the underside of a ladybug. The wasp injects an egg. Along with the egg, she inserts a virus. The virus paralyzes the ladybug.

virus—a germ that infects living things and causes diseases

paralyze—to cause a loss of the ability to control the muscles

Inside the ladybug, the wasp egg hatches into a larva. The larva gobbles up its host's digested food. Three weeks later, the fattened-up larva bursts out of its ladybug home. Even with the larva out of its body, the ladybug remains under its control. Instead of fleeing, the ladybug stands still. The larva spins a cocoon between the ladybug's legs. The host protects the pupa from predators. A week later an adult wasp crawls out of its cocoon.

wasp cocoon between the legs of a ladybug

No longer needed, the ladybug drops dead.

Parasitoid Wasps and Stinging Wasps

Parasitoid wasps rarely, if ever, sting people. It's the nonparasitic ones that send us running for cover. Parasitoid wasps, on the other hand, can be helpful to humans. They eat bugs that feast on crops.

THE ZOMBIE-MAKING HAIRWORM

Grasshoppers, crickets, and praying mantises avoid water. Why? They can't swim!

But when a tiny HAIRWORM sneaks inside their body, everything changes.

The cycle begins when a hairworm egg hatches in water. The young larva first works its way into a mosquito's body. Soon a grasshopper, cricket, or mantis eats the mosquito—with the hairworm larva inside. The hairworm larva rapidly grows inside its new home. Then the larva eats everything non-vital inside its host. It needs its host to stay alive—for now!

hairworm—a long, slender parasitic worm, also called a nematode

When it's ready to come out, the hairworm's mind-controlling begins. It steers its host toward a lake or stream.

There, the grasshopper, cricket, or praying mantis uncontrollably plunges to its death.

The hairworm slithers out of its host. Then it swims off to find mates.

hairworm exiting a praying mantis in water

FAST FACT The hairworm grows three to 10 times longer than its host. It lives curled up inside until it's time to come out.

ZOMBIE BEETLES

parasitic tapeworm

Found in grain silos and flour warehouses all over the world, dwarf tapeworms start their lives as eggs in rat poop. The smell of the eggy poop is irresistible to beetles. The insects munch away on the poop. Once inside a beetle, a tapeworm egg hatches into a larva.

The larva grows hooks to claw its way around inside.

tapeworm—a parasitic flatworm with a soft, flat body

Normally a beetle hides in a pile of grain or flour. But just like a zombie, this tapeworm-infected beetle is no longer in control. It slowly wanders around the surface of the pile. A normal beetle also defends itself by letting out a bad smell. Predators avoid the stinky beetle. However, the crafty tapeworm stops the beetle from making the smell.

The tapeworm isn't finished yet. It releases chemicals.

flour beetle

The chemicals make nearby rats attracted to the beetle. Soon a rat gobbles down the beetle. Now inside the rat, the tapeworm grows into an adult. It makes more eggs. The eggs come out with the rat's poop. More beetles come along to munch away.

ZOMBIE-MAKING THORNY-HEADED WORMS

Grammarids are tiny shrimplike creatures. They normally avoid the surface of the waters they live in. Here their predators loom. Instead these creatures hide near the bottom.

That is until thorny-headed worms get inside their body.

grammarid with thorny-headed worm larva (orange circle) inside of it

Grammarids feed on eggs, including eggs of the thorny-headed worm. The worm eggs hatch inside the grammarids. Tiny larvae begin to grow—and take control of their hosts. The grammarids travel like zombies to waters they usually avoid.

FAST FACT The thorny-headed worm is also called a spiny-headed worm. It is named for hooks that hold it in place when inside its host. The grippers work so well that humans have copied their design to create a new type of medical tape.

In these waters the grammarids have many bird predators. The birds eat the grammarids. Now in a new bird home, the thorny-headed worms finish growing. Then they lay eggs. The eggs come out in the bird's poop. Then more unlucky grammarids come along to eat, starting the cycle over.

THE ZOMBIE STICKLEBACK FISH

There's another tapeworm that is a clever mind-controller. It enlists the help of three different hosts.

stickleback fish

The tapeworm begins its body-snatching scheme as a free-swimming adult. A copepod eats the tapeworm. Then a stickleback fish eats the copepod.

The tapeworm is still alive inside the fish.

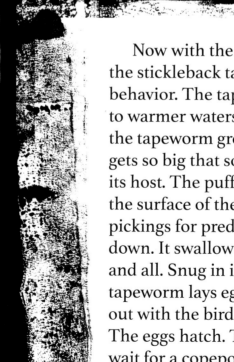

Now with the worm inside it, the stickleback takes on zombielike behavior. The tapeworm steers the fish to warmer waters. The warmth helps the tapeworm grow. The tapeworm gets so big that sometimes it outweighs its host. The puffed up fish rises to the surface of the water. It is now easy pickings for predators. A bird swoops down. It swallows the fish, tapeworm and all. Snug in its new home, the tapeworm lays eggs. The eggs come out with the bird's poop into the water. The eggs hatch. The new tapeworms wait for a copepod to eat them.

copepod—a small freshwater or marine animal

ZOMBIE KILLIFISH

Along the coast of California, a horn snail feasts on bird poop. Little does the snail know, the poop is full of fluke eggs.

Now inside the snail, the eggs hatch into larvae. The larvae work their way out of the snail and into the water. They swim off in search of their next host, the killifish.

A fluke larva latches onto a killifish's gills. Then it finds its way inside. It crawls through the fish's body to the brain, causing it to act strangely.

killifish

fluke—a type of parasitic flatworm

Like an out-of-control zombie, the fish hops, jumps, and shimmies.

Shorebirds are 10 to 30 times more likely to snatch up one of the dancing killifish than one of its uninfected peers. Gulp! A shorebird eats a tasty fish, and the fluke is now happily inside the bird. In its new bird home, the fluke lays eggs. The eggs come out in the bird's poop. A nearby snail is waiting to eat the eggy poop, and the cycle starts over.

FAST FACT

The *kill* in *killifish* might send shivers down your spine. However, this little minnow got its name from the Dutch word *kilde*. It means "small stream" or "puddle."

Soon these body snatchers are at work zombifying their next victim!

ZOMBIE-MAKING LANCET LIVER FLUKES

lancet liver fluke

Lancet liver flukes begin their lives as eggs in the poop of a grazing sheep, cow, or pig. A hungry snail eats the poop. Larvae hatch from the eggs.

The snail coughs out slimy balls of the larvae.

graze—to feed on growing grass or herbs

An ant eats **the slim**y larvae. The larvae move straight to the **ant's brain**. Here they start their zombie-making **work**. Instead of returning to its mound at night, **the a**nt climbs a stalk of grass for all to see. Here **it's** more likely to be eaten—exactly as the **larvae p**lanned.

If no predators show up, the **ant** returns to "normal" during **the** day. The larvae need to keep **their** host from baking in the **day**time sun. But the next night, **the** ant again climbs to the top **of a** blade of grass. A grazing **mammal** swallows the ant along **with** a bite grass. The flukes **make** their way to the animal's **liver.** They grow into adults and **lay e**ggs. The eggs come out **in the** grazing animal's poop. **Anoth**er snail eats the poop, **starting** the cycle again.

Mind-controlling parasites abound in nature. The next time you see something acting strangely, beware! A body snatcher may be behind this creature's zombielike behavior.

GLOSSARY

burrow (BUHR-oh)—a hole in the ground made or used by an animal

copepod (COPE-pod)—a small freshwater or marine animal

fluke (FLUKE)—a type of parasitic flatworm

graze (GRAYZ)—to feed on growing grass or herbs

hairworm (HARE-worm)—a long, slender parasitic worm, also called a nematode

host (HOHST)—a living plant or animal on which a parasite lives

larva (LAR-vuh)—a stage of an insect's life between egg and adult

life cycle (LIFE SYE-kuhl)—the series of changes a living thing goes through from birth to death

molt (MOLT)—to shed an outer layer of skin

paralyze (PARE-uh-lize)—to cause a loss of the ability to control the muscles

parasite (PAIR-uh-site)—an animal or plant that lives on or inside another animal or plant

parasitoid (PAIR-uh-sit-ouid)—a parasite that kills its host

pesticide (PES-tuh-side)—a poisonous chemical used to kill insects, rats, and fungi that can damage plants

predator (PRED-uh-tur)—an animal that hunts other animals for food

pupate (PYOO-pate)—the process in which an insect changes from a larva into an adult

swarm (SWARM)—to gather or fly close together in a large group

tapeworm (TAYP-worm)—a parasitic flatworm with a soft, flat body

venom (VEN-uhm)—a poisonous liquid produced by some animals

virus (VYE-ruhss)—a germ that infects living things and causes diseases

vital organ (VYE-tuhl OR-guhn)—a body part needed to stay alive

READ MORE

Hirschmann, Kris. *Real Life Zombies.* New York: Scholastic, 2013.

Johnson, Rebecca L. *Zombie Makers: True Stories of Nature's Undead.* Minneapolis, Minn.: Millbrook Press, 2013.

Larson, Kirsten W. *Zombies in Nature.* Freaky Nature. Mankato, Minn.: Amicus Ink, 2016.

INTERNET SITES

FactHound offers a safe, fun way to find Internet sites related to this book. All of the sites on FactHound have been researched by our staff.

Here's all you do:

Visit *www.facthound.com*

Type in this code: 9781515724803

 Check out projects, games and lots more at **www.capstonekids.com**

INDEX